This book belongs to...
Ce livre est la propriété de...

Geoffrey. B.

Editor
Stephen Attmore

Artists
John Blackman and Mandy Doyle
Tony Gibbons
Terry Hadler
Bob Hersey
Eric Kincaid
Jack Pelling
Brian Watson

Cover design by Sebastian Quigley

Acknowledgements

Susan Griggs Agency: 15C, 19TL, 45R, 52BL/BR, 53TL, 54TL/TC/TR, 55T, 57; **VISION INTERNATIONAL**: (M. Mann) 15T, (G. Blond) 22L, (A. Driver) 23C, (P. Koch) 56; **ZEFA**: 19TR, 45TL/BL,53R; **Popperfoto**: 22R; **Sporting Pictures (UK) Ltd**: 23B; **Shell photograph**: 28; **Novosti Press Agency**: 33TL/TR; **NASA**: 33BL/57T; **The RAF Falcons**: 36; **RAF**: 37T; **Picturepoint – LONDON**: 37BR; **Colorific**: (D. Hunt) 37BL; **Associated Press**: 39; **London Express News and Feature Services**: 41; **Japan Tourist Organisation**: 44; **Science Photo Library**: (J. Walsh) 46T, (W. M. McIntyre) 46BL; **Heffers Printers Ltd**: 46BL; **'Flight International'**: 47, 68TL, 72; **Sonia Halliday**: 52TL; **Barnaby's Picture Library**: 52TR; **ARDEA LONDON**: (J. Mason) 53BL, (R. Bunge) 54BR; **The Photo Source**: 54BL, 66B; **Planet Earth Pictures/SEAPHOT**: 60; **U S Treasury**: 66T, 68BL; **British Tourist Authority**: 68TR; **The J. Allan Cash Photolibrary**: 68BR; © **Crown**: 70; 73 – reproduced with kind permission of the Controller of Her Majesty's Stationery Office. 14TR/L – used by kind permission of Tesco Training Services

PEOPLE
and the
MAN-MADE WORLD

Karen O'Callaghan

BRIMAX BOOKS·NEWMARKET·ENGLAND

Introduction

This book provides an opportunity for children to discover interesting and unusual facts about people and cultures around the world. Children will learn how men and women have made astonishing conquests over nature; how they have designed and built incredible structures and created machines that affect all our lives.

There are two main sections – PEOPLE and the MAN-MADE WORLD. These are subdivided to cover: *on the land* – from police around the world to famous buildings; *in the water* – from working under the sea to special ships; and *in the air* – from people's early attempts at flying to spacecraft.

The section on PEOPLE is varied and interesting. It includes information on contrasting customs, different environments and backgrounds. The MAN-MADE WORLD section deals with modern technology, ranging from computers to trains, from oil rigs to aircraft. All countries mentioned in the book are shown on a double-page map of the world. This helps readers to build up an overall picture with a constant reference.

This book will excite children's natural curiosity and imagination. It will stimulate interest in acquiring further knowledge about the world around them. More than 200 superb pictures bring the book to life. The text is designed for young readers and the book covers an interest level for children from 5 to 10 years.

ISBN 0 86112 361 1

© BRIMAX BOOKS LTD 1986. All rights reserved
Published by Brimax Books, Newmarket, England 1986
Printed in Hungary

Contents

PEOPLE

On the land

There are millions of people all over the world, and each of us is different. We come in many shapes, sizes and colours. The countries that we live in can be hot, cold, wet or dry. We wear different clothes to suit where we live.

China

Polynesia

India

Russia

Mexico

Iceland

USA

Nigeria

The **shortest woman** is 61 cm (24 inches). The **shortest man** is 67 cm (26½ inches).

The **average height** for a man is 178 cm (5 ft 10 in). The average height for a woman is 165 cm (5 ft 5 in).

The **tallest man** is 272 cm (8 feet 11 inches) and the **tallest woman** is 246 cm (8 feet 1 inch).

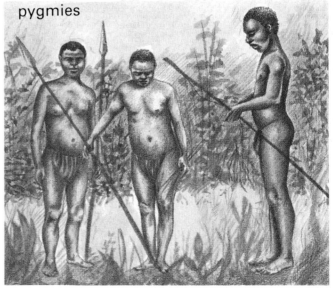

pygmies

The **tallest group of people** are the herdsmen of Rwanda and Burundi. They come from Central Africa.

The **shortest group of people** are the Mbuti pygmies. They live in the forests of Zaire in Africa.

Different ideas of beauty

All over the world people decorate themselves. In different countries, the ideas of what is beautiful are not always the same.

Some tribes in Africa decorate their ears. Children have their ears pierced when they are seven. Small discs are forced inside the holes, to stretch them. As the skin stretches, larger discs are used, until the skin is stretched around a huge decorated earring.

Women of the **Padaung tribe** in Burma wear brass rings around their necks. When a Padaung girl is five the first ring is put around her neck. As she gets older, more rings are added. They are very heavy. Some weigh 9 kg (20 lbs).

It is the men of the **Wodaabe tribe** in Africa that make themselves beautiful. They lighten their skins with a special powder and paint their faces. Then the men stand in a circle and the women choose their husbands.

Ways of greeting

There are many countries in the world. People from each country have their own ideas and customs. They have different ideas of what to wear, what looks nice, and what is polite.

In **India** the polite way to greet each other is to join hands, like praying.

In **Russia** people hug each other.

In **Japan** people bow to each other.

In **France** it is the custom to kiss each other on both cheeks.

In **Germany** and many other countries, business men and women shake hands.

In **Alaska** the Innuit (Eskimos) rub noses when they say 'hello'.

Schools

Children all over the world go to school, but schools are not always the same. Many children living in hot countries have lessons outside.

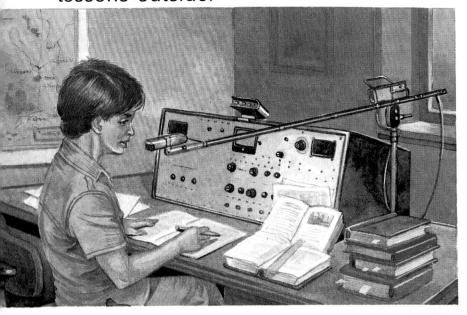

Some Australian children do not go to a school. They live far from towns, in the outback. In the morning they have lessons over a two-way radio. It is called the 'School of the Air'. In the afternoon they do homework, which is posted to their teacher. They meet the teacher and the other children once a year at a special summer school.

Some boys living in Nepal go to special schools at the age of 5, to train as monks. They get up very early, at 5 a.m. There is an hour of prayer and meditation before lessons begin.

In **Russia** some children as young as three years old, go to special music schools. They have lessons and learn to play musical instruments.

Children in Tanzania
(Africa) start school very early in the morning. The village craftsmen – basketmakers, potters, weavers and carpenters – teach the children their skills. The children grow maize and groundnuts in the school garden. They make this into a thick porridge, and eat it for their school dinner.

School children in Tokyo
(Japan) play games and sports on the flat roof of the school building. It is such a crowded city that schools do not have playgrounds or playing fields.

Chinese children
have exercises every day before lessons. This helps to keep them fit, strong and healthy.

Shopping

Many countries in the western world have **hypermarkets**. These are enormous shops, often as big as a football field. All kinds of food, household goods and clothes are sold there. They are usually built outside towns and have large car parks.

In Bangladesh many goods are sold from stalls in **open markets**. It is the custom here, that all the stall holders are men. The women work in the villages.

In Japan most people **shop every day** at local shops and street markets. They like to buy food fresh every day, rather than stock up food for a week or more.

This **market** in Thailand is **on the river**. Some people come in small boats and others come to the water's edge to buy fruit and vegetables.

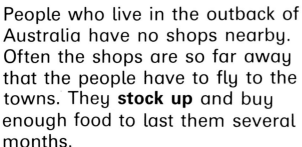

People who live in the outback of Australia have no shops nearby. Often the shops are so far away that the people have to fly to the towns. They **stock up** and buy enough food to last them several months.

In America and Canada there are **shopping malls**. Many kinds of shops and restaurants are under one roof. Many of the shops have no doors. Whatever the weather outside, it is always dry and warm inside.

Different ways of living

People's lives can be very different. Some countries are rich, some countries are poor.

Los Angeles, in America, is called **'car city'**. Most of the people have cars and they go everywhere in them. They have drive-in banks, movies, shops and even drive-in churches. At drive-in restaurants people sit in their cars to eat.

Many houses in Japan **do not have bathrooms**. Families go to the public bath house to wash. Here there are many large baths with taps around the edge. It is a meeting place. People relax and soak in the water with their friends.

In parts of China, farm workers cannot afford their own television set. Villagers **share one television**. This is watched by as many as 25 families in a large hall.

In Ghana (Africa), villagers **do not have tap water** in their houses. Hundreds of people share one tap. Women bring washing here and carry water back home.

Inside some houses

Bedouin people live in the deserts of Arabia and North Africa. They **live in tents** made with goatskin pieces woven together. The tent has two rooms. The back room is used for cooking and sleeping. The front room is used to entertain visitors.

In the rain forests of Borneo, many families **live together in one long house**. The house is 70 metres (230 feet) wide. There are no inside walls. Each family has its own section, with areas for cooking, washing, eating and sleeping.

In Japan, **houses are very small**. A family of five may have only two small rooms divided by a sliding paper door. They use the same room to live and sleep in. Bedding is rolled up and put away during the day. It is spread out on the floor at night.

Houses

People build houses with the materials that are around them. The kind of house depends upon the weather in that area.

This house is in **Iran** where it is **very hot**. It has no windows. There is only a small opening near the top of the wind tower. Any breeze there is goes down the tower into the house. Thick walls keep it cool inside.

This house is in **Norway** where it is **very cold**. The house is built on a layer of stones to keep it dry. The roof is covered with turf and tree bark. It is very steep so that snow falls off easily.

This house is in **Darwin**, Australia, where it is **very windy**. It was built around a central pillar. When a cyclone (storm) comes, the house sways but it is not blown down.

This house is in **India**, where it is **very wet**. The walls are made of bamboo, covered with thick mud. The roof of rice straw is very steep so that rain runs off quickly.

In **Calcutta** (India) the people are very poor. Their houses are made of cardboard boxes and scraps of metal. They are called **shanty towns**.

Many people in **Singapore** live in **blocks of flats**. These take up less space in this crowded city. They have no gardens, so the people hang washing out of the windows on poles.

On **Madeira Island** (near Africa) the roofs of the houses are thatched and they slope down to the ground.

In **northern Tunisia** (Africa) some people live in **caves**. People who live in caves are called troglodytes. The rooms are cool in the summer and warm in winter.

19

Police around the world

Every country has a police force. They all wear uniforms to show the job they do.

USA   India   France   Britain

Saudi Arabia   Papua New Guinea   Canada

Working underground

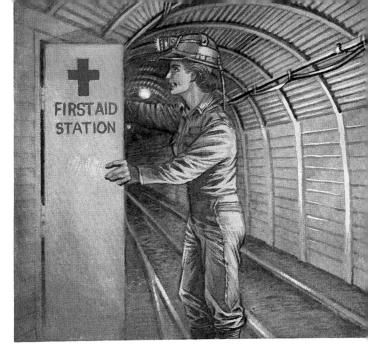

This man is a **coal-face machine driver**. The machine cuts away coal from the coal-face. It weighs 17 tonnes. He cuts out about 150 tonnes of coal every day.

This woman is a **colliery nurse**. She goes down the mine to check the first-aid equipment. Each mine has several First-Aid Stations that have medical equipment to deal with emergencies.

These **gold miners** are carried down into the mine in a steel cage. It travels down through a shaft 1·6 km (1 mile) deep in two minutes. The gold is mined 4 km (2½ miles) below the surface. It is very hot in the gold mines. To keep them cool the men wear special jackets with pockets filled with ice. After a few hours they change their jacket for a new one from the deep freeze.

'A race to the finish'

The **rarajipari**, or **kickball race**, takes place in South America. Two teams of Tarahumara Indians race each other, to kick a wooden ball across mountainous countryside. They wear rattles on their bodies to keep them awake. The race may last several days and cover up to 322 km (200 miles).

The **Iditarod** is the world's longest dog sled race. The course is 1600 km (1000 miles) long, from Anchorage to Nome, in Alaska. Winds of 128 km/h (80 mph), temperatures 45° below zero and snowstorms make this a very difficult race. Only nine of this woman's 15 dogs survived the race. She was suffering from frost-bite as she came to the finish. It had taken her 16 days.

The **Tour de France** is a 25-day cycle race. The riders stop at night and start again in the morning. The course is 4800 km (3000 miles).

Hundreds of people run in the **London Marathon**, but not all finish. The course is 42·2 km (26 miles 385 yds) long. The fastest time is 2 hr 7 m 11 s.

Sports

The world's fastest ball game is **pelota**. It is played in Mexico. The two players have scoops strapped to their arms. The hard elastic ball is caught in the scoop and tossed out. It travels at lightning speed against the walls of the court. The ball can travel at 320 km/h (200 mph).

Sumo wrestling is the oldest sport in Japan. The wrestlers are very fat and heavy. They eat huge meals to put on extra weight. The contest lasts only a few minutes. The winner is the wrestler who throws his opponent to the ground out of the ring.

Soccer is the most popular football sport. It is played in nearly every country in the world. Many countries compete for the famous World Cup. The finals are held every four years.

23

In the water
Sports

Cave diving is a dangerous sport. The divers explore underground rivers and caves. They have lights on their helmets to help them find their way in the darkness.

Target divers dive from a height of 40 m (130 ft). The tank has a target painted on the bottom and each diver tries to hit the bull's-eye.

Water polo is a team sport played in many countries. Each team has seven players. The players swim, dribble and pass the ball. They can catch or throw the ball using only one hand.

In **ski-kiting** the skier holds a large, light kite. As the skier is towed along at speed, she is lifted into the air. She can glide for several minutes before landing.

In **ski-jumping** a boat is driven in a straight line about 5 m (15 feet) to the right of a jumping ramp. The skier is pulled up the ramp and takes off into the air. Good jumpers can soar many metres through the air and land safely.

Race walking is a sport in Polynesia. A course is marked out on the seabed, using wooden pegs. It is about 63 m (70 yds) long. The walkers carry a heavy stone to keep them under the water. They are not allowed to swim. They must walk the course. The water is very clear and they are watched by people in boats on the surface.

Houses above water

In **Thailand** some people live in **houses built on stilts**. They have flooded their land so that they can grow rice and catch fish.

In **Peru**, people live on Lake Titicaca which is the highest inland sea in the world. By planting totara reeds they have made islands. The reeds grow down 1·8 m (6 ft) into the water. The people build their huts on top of the reeds. The totara reed is used for many things – building huts and making boats, bedmats and baskets.

In **Hong Kong** there is a **floating village** called Aberdeen. There are 4000 boats, shops and temples. Families live on boats called junks. Other boats called sampans are used for fishing.

Houses under water

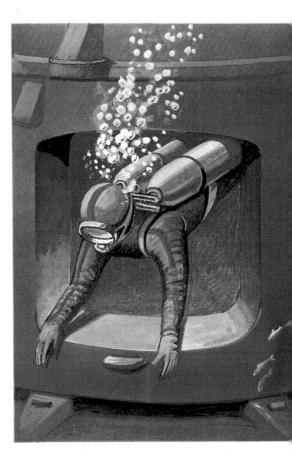

the underwater hatch
(door) into Tektite

Tektite is an American experimental craft. It was built to see
how long people can live and work under the sea. It was
lowered 15 metres (50 feet) into the sea. Crews of divers
lived in Tektite for eight weeks.

Hydrolab is another
American underwater
habitat (home).
People living under
the sea are called
aquanauts. Hydrolab
rests on the seabed.
The teams of divers
explore and carry
out experiments.

Working under the sea

Film companies employ **underwater cameramen and women**. They use special waterproof cameras. This skin diver is filming a coral reef and the animals that live there. She breathes air through tubes from an aqualung strapped on her back. She is working 10 m (30 feet) down. The air in the tank will last for about 40 minutes.

inside a JIM su

This is a **deep-sea diver**. He is wearing a strong diving suit called a JIM. With this suit on, a deep-sea diver can work 500 m (1640 ft) down and can stay under water for a long time. Out of the water, the suit weighs half a tonne. However, the diver can move about easily under the water. With the special metal hands of the suit, the diver can pick up small objects.

Pearl divers collect oysters from the seabed. They are found about 15–30 m (50–100 ft) below the surface. They do not wear breathing equipment, but can hold their breath for several minutes. They carry sharp knives to cut the oysters away from the coral. It is difficult and dangerous work. There are many sharks in these warm Pacific waters.

One diver is **mending an oil pipeline** under the sea. The other diver is checking the pipe. He uses a scuba scooter to pull himself along through the water.

Unusual ways of fishing

Some **tribes in South America** have a special way of catching fish. They collect poisonous plants, crush them and put them in a basket in the river. The poison is carried downstream in the water. The poison makes the fish sleepy and they swim very slowly. Then it is easy for the men to spear and catch the fish.

These **Japanese fishermen** use birds to help them catch fish. Cormorants are tied to the small boat. They dive down into the water, bringing the fish up in their beaks. Rope is tied round their necks so that they cannot swallow the fish. The men fish at night and the light from lanterns attracts fish to the boat.

Some fishermen in Canada fish from inside a hut, on a frozen lake. The hut has a hole in the floor. A hole is cut through the ice. The fisherman sits and dangles his line through the hole in the floor, into the water.

Emergency services

The Navy and Air Force work closely with the Coastguards to provide a search and rescue service. All the crews wear lifejackets and carry medical equipment. It is a dangerous job as rescues often take place in rough seas and stormy weather.

This boy fell down a cliff. A large lifeboat cannot get near the cliff, so an **inflatable lifeboat** is used. The boy is badly hurt. He is strapped to a stretcher. Then he is winched up into the **RAF rescue helicopter** and taken to hospital.

This ship has sent a distress signal to the Coastguard. She is in danger of sinking. A **lifeboat** and a **Navy Sea King helicopter** have come to the rescue. The helicopter uses its powerful searchlights to light up the sea. Many people clamber aboard the lifeboat. Others are on a life-raft. They are winched up, one by one, into the safety of the helicopter.

In the air

Emergency services

In Australia there is a **flying doctor service**. Many people live on farms which are miles from the nearest town. They call for help, in an emergency, using a two-way radio. The planes have room for one stretcher patient, a sitting patient, the doctor and the pilot. Anyone seriously ill is flown to the nearest hospital.

In America they have a new emergency service called **para-rescue**. People are dropped by parachute, to help anyone in trouble. They are trained in many skills because they deal with many different kinds of emergency. They are taught parachuting, first-aid, mountaineering, arctic survival and skin diving.

Space

The **first man in Space** was Yuri Gagarin. He was a Russian Air Force major. In 1961 he orbited the earth in his spacecraft 'Vostok I'.

The **first woman in Space** was Valentina Tereshkova. She travelled in 'Vostok II' in 1963. The Russians call their people in Space **cosmonauts**.

The **first man on the Moon** was Neil Armstrong. He took this photograph of the second man to step on to the Moon, Edwin Aldrin. They landed on the Moon in 1969 and collected samples (pieces) of moon rock. Americans call their people in Space **astronauts**.

The first **free-flight in Space** was made by Captain McCandless and Lieutenant Colonel Stewart in 1984. They were on a mission in the Space Shuttle 'Challenger'. They wore special back packs, which have 24 gas jets to move them around.

Living in Space

The Earth pulls everything towards it. The pull (or force) is called **gravity**. In Space there is no gravity and everything floats. This makes living in Space very different and sometimes difficult.

Eating and drinking – food comes ready made in plastic packs. If it is dry, they squirt water into the bag to mix the food. They squirt drinks into their mouths through a tube.

Sleeping – astronauts have special beds fixed to the walls. They sleep upright, strapped into their sleeping bags.

Exercise – it is important to exercise. Inside the spacecraft they have special pedalling machines.

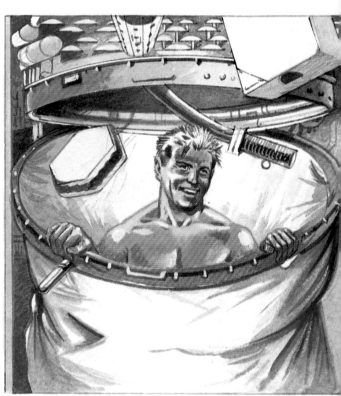

Washing – astronauts shower inside a special bag that is fixed to the ceiling.

Spacesuits – if astronauts leave the spacecraft, they must wear a special spacesuit. This protects them from the heat of the Sun's rays and the freezing cold of Space. Inside the suit is air for them to breathe and a radio so that they can talk to the others.

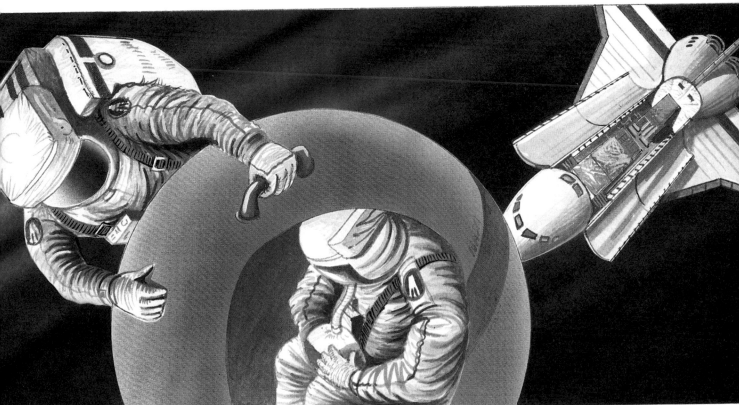

Rescue – if all the astronauts have to leave their spacecraft in an emergency, two of them wear spacesuits. The others are zipped into special rescue balls. These are carried to a rescue ship.

Sports

Every year in early May, people in Thailand and Japan have **kite fights**. They tie razor blades and broken glass on to the edges of kites. The huge kites are flown by a team. They try to cut up the other team's kite. The winners are the team whose kite is left in the air.

Hang gliding is a world-wide sport. The gliders use rising air currents and the wind to keep them up. The person can change direction by moving his or her body from side to side.

Sky-diving – these sky-divers jump from an aircraft flying at around 3000 m (10,000 feet). They fall through the air, making patterns in the sky. They will only open their parachutes when they are about 900 m (3000 feet) from the ground.

Flying displays

Many countries have flying aerobatic display teams. The planes make patterns in the sky and show us the great skill of the pilots. The patterns are called formations.

The British team is called the **Red Arrows**.

different formations

The **Thunderbirds** are the American team.

The **Snowbirds** are the Canadian team.

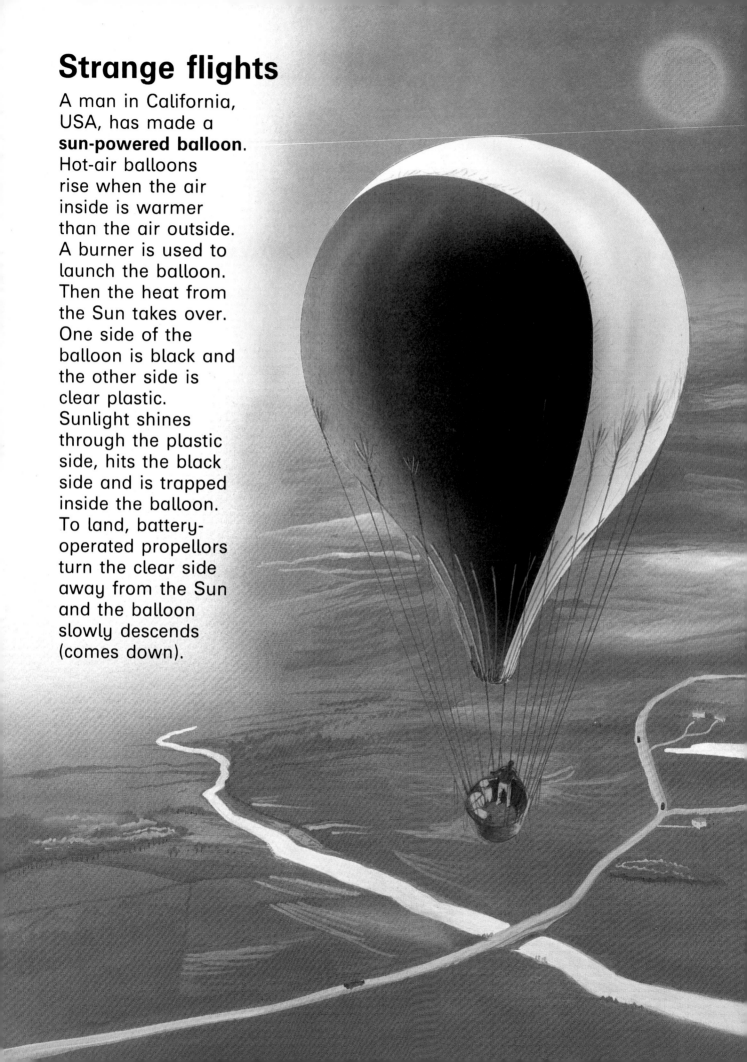

Strange flights

A man in California, USA, has made a **sun-powered balloon**. Hot-air balloons rise when the air inside is warmer than the air outside. A burner is used to launch the balloon. Then the heat from the Sun takes over. One side of the balloon is black and the other side is clear plastic. Sunlight shines through the plastic side, hits the black side and is trapped inside the balloon. To land, battery-operated propellors turn the clear side away from the Sun and the balloon slowly descends (comes down).

Four men made a **balloon flight across the Pacific Ocean** in 1981. They flew in a balloon called 'Double Eagle V', from Japan to California, USA. They travelled 9282 km (5768 miles) across the Pacific Ocean. It took them four days and five nights. They tried to reach a height of 7925 km (26,000 feet), but it was so cold that ice formed on the balloon and they had to fly lower.

In 1982 this man flew across the English Channel in a flying machine called **Gossamer Albatross**. It weighs 34 kg (75 lbs) and has no engine. The only source of power is its pedals. It took three hours to cover the 33½ km (21 miles) across the Channel.

Setting a goal

On land, in water and in the air, people risk their lives to set new records. Often these adventures are very dangerous.

Two men set out to **climb a frozen waterfall** in Switzerland. It was 152 m (500 ft) high. They used ice axes and shoes with sharp spikes to dig into the ice. Part of the climb was up a curtain of ice which hung clear of the rock. They finished the climb before warmer weather set in and the ice melted.

This **long-distance swimmer** from India achieved four incredible swims in one year. In April he swam the Palk Strait from India to Sri Lanka. In August he swam across the Strait of Gibraltar, from Europe to Africa. In September he swam the Dardanelles, from Europe to Turkey. In October he swam the entire length of the Panama Canal. His name is Mihir Sen.

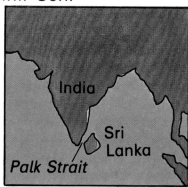

India

Sri Lanka

Palk Strait

EUROPE

Strait of Gibraltar

AFRICA

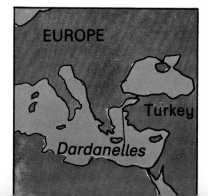

EUROPE

Turkey

Dardanelles

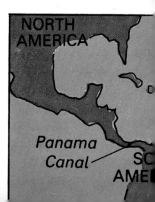

NORTH AMERICA

Panama Canal

SC AME

This **hot-air balloon** was called 'Explorer II'. In 1935 this giant balloon went up to a height of 22 km (72,395 feet) above the Earth. It was the highest anyone had ever been. This record lasted for 22 years. Since 1935 many people have ascended (gone up) to greater heights. Now hot-air balloons go up to the edge of Space. When people go this high they wear special pressure suits, like astronauts.

This woman **sailed round the world single-handed** (on her own), in her yacht 'Express Crusader'. Her name is Naomi Lewis. She covered 48,278 km (30,000 miles) in nine months. She travelled 209 km (130 miles) every day.

Alaska
Anchorage
Canada
Vancouver
Columbia River
California
USA
Chicago
New York
San Francisco
Washington
Maryland
Carolina
Los Angeles
New Orleans
· Bermuda
Mexico
West Indies
Virgin Islands
Peru
SOUTH
AMERICA

Iceland
North Sea
Norway
Great
Britain
EUR
London
German
English Channel
Italy
Paris
France
Madeira island
Tunisia
AFRIC
Ghana
Za

The South Pole – Antarctic

South Pole

key

	sea
	snow
	desert
	plains
	forests, jungles

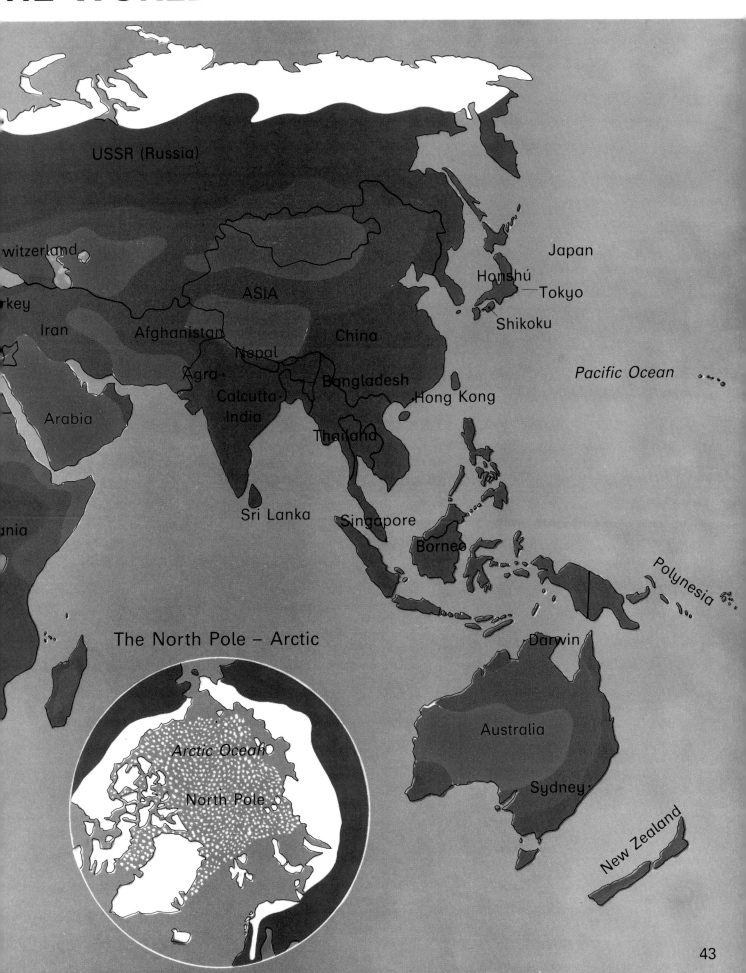

USSR (Russia)

witzerland

Japan

Honshú

Tokyo

ASIA

rkey

Shikoku

Iran

Afghanistan

China

Pacific Ocean

Nepal

Agra

Bangladesh

Calcutta

Hong Kong

Arabia

India

Thailand

ania

Sri Lanka

Singapore

Polynesia

Borneo

Darwin

The North Pole – Arctic

Australia

Arctic Ocean

North Pole

Sydney

New Zealand

MAN-MADE WORLD
On the land

The St Gotthard **road tunnel** in Switzerland is the longest road tunnel in the world. It is 16·32 km (10·14 miles) long. It has two lanes of traffic and it runs from Göschenen to Airolo.

Tokyo is the biggest city in the world. It is in Japan. There are 11 million people living and working there.

'**Thrust 2**' is the fastest jet engine on wheels. This car achieved the land speed record, in the Nevada desert, USA, in 1984. It travelled at a speed of 1035 km/h (643 mph). It is the fastest British car.

The United States of America is the **country with the most roads**. They have more than 6,000,000 km (3,728,400 miles) of roadway. The fastest roads are called freeways. In different countries, fast roads have different names: in France – autoroute; Germany – autobahn; Italy – autostrada; England – motorway. The Los Angeles Freeway carries traffic quickly through the city.

Venice, in Italy, is the only city in the world that has no roads. It has only footpaths and canals.

The **Sears Tower** in Chicago, USA, is the tallest office building in the world. It is 443 m (1454 feet) high. There are 110 floors (storeys) with 16,700 people working there. It has 103 elevators, 18 escalators and 16,000 windows.

How we use computers

Computers are a great help to us. They can work very fast and do many jobs at once. They have made new inventions possible.

Microcomputers are the smallest computers. Scientists found they could print electronic circuits on to a single, tiny chip of silicon. These **microprocessors** work faster. Some silicon chips are used for memory, to store information. Microprocessors are found in pocket calculators, digital watches and desk-top computers. They also control many machines and electronic toys. We can program the cooker to switch itself on and off.

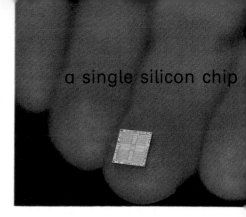

a single silicon chip

digital watch

automatic cooker

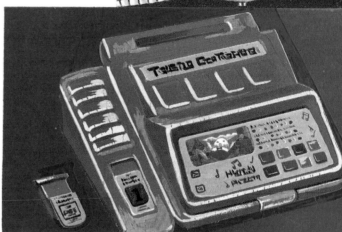

electronic toy

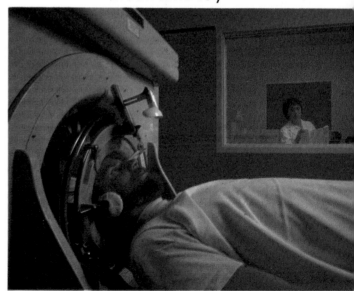

Newspaper and magazine printers use computers to arrange the text (writing) and the pictures on a page, ready for printing.

Hospitals use computers. X-ray scanners take many pictures. The computer sorts them and shows them on a television screen.

The **Police** use computers to control traffic lights in busy cities. In the central control room, the Police can watch out for traffic jams.

The **underground railway** in San Francisco (USA) is controlled by a computer system. It is called BART (the Bay Area Rapid Transit system). There is no driver.

Flight simulators are used to train airline pilots. Inside the simulator it feels as if you are flying in an aircraft. The huge machine is on legs. A computer makes the legs move. Instead of windows there are television screens. The computer can show pictures on these of all the main airports around the world, day or night. This means pilots can practise landing an aircraft.

This **car factory** uses robots which are controlled by computers. The robots do paint spraying and welding jobs. They can work very quickly. They can weld (join) the metal in 250 places in 23 seconds.

Trains

The **fastest train** in the world is the French TGV. It travels between Paris and Lyon at 298 km/h (185 mph). It is so fast that it needs 3·2 km (2 miles) to slow down and stop.

In Wuppertal in West Germany there is a **monorail**. This is a train that hangs down from an overhead rail. The track is 20 m (65½ feet) above the ground.

In Birmingham, England, there is a new **magnetic train**, called Mag-Lev. There are four pairs of magnets on each side of the train which lift it 15 mm (⅗ inch) above the track.

The Metro train at Lille, France, is an **underground train**. It is controlled by computer. There is no driver or guard. Passengers get their tickets from machines.

Cable railways have
no engines. They are
pulled up and down steep
slopes by cables. There are
two tracks, side by side.
As one train comes down, the
other one is pulled up.

Mountain railways are called rack
and pinion railways. They run on
a special track. A third rail in the
middle of the track has teeth on
it. A wheel under the train also
has teeth. This is the **pinion**. The
teeth fit into the **rack** on the track.
This stops the train slipping backwards.

The railway up Mount Pilatus in
Switzerland is the steepest **rack
and pinion** railway in the world.
Inside the cars, the seats go up
in steps. This stops the people
from falling out of their seats
as the train goes up the steep
mountainside.

Monster machines

This **house-mover** is a **lift rig** weighing 200 tonnes. It picks up houses that are to be moved and takes them to a new place.

The **Arctic Snow Train** has 54 wheels and is the longest vehicle ever built. It is 174·3 m (572 feet) long and has a top speed of 32 km/h (20 mph).

This is the **longest bus in the world**. It works in the Middle East oil-fields, carrying people to work. It is 23 m (76 feet) long. It can carry 187 passengers (121 sitting and 66 standing).

This **transporter** (right) was built to carry space rockets. It is 39·9 m (131 ft) long, 35 m (114 ft) wide and 6 m (20 ft) high. It moves at a speed of 1·6 km/h (1 mph).

This **mining dump truck** can carry 77,000 kg (76 tons) of rock and earth. Its engine is as powerful as 11 cars. It has seven forward and one reverse (backward) gears.

Big Muskie is a dragline excavator. It works in open cast mines. A small house would fit inside its huge bucket, which holds 200,000 kg (1968 tonnes).

Famous buildings – old and new

The **Taj Mahal** at Agra in India took 20 years to build. Its white marble walls have been carved by hand and inlaid with patterns using semi-precious stones. Shah Jahan ordered it to be built as a memory to his young wife when she died. It is surrounded by gardens.

The **Great Pyramid** at Giza in Egypt was built over 4500 years ago. One hundred thousand slaves moved and lifted more than two million stone slabs to build the pyramid. It took 30 years to complete. Inside there are chambers where the Pharaohs and Queens were buried.

The **Great Wall of China** was built in the third century BC (Before Christ). It is 6325 km (3930 miles) long, 12 m (39 feet) high and 10 m (32 feet) thick. The Great Wall is the only man-made structure that can be seen from Space.

The **Leaning Tower of Pisa**, in Italy, has eight storeys. When the builders reached the third storey it began to lean over. This may be because it was built on sand. They finished building it, but each year it leans over more. One day it may fall down.

The **Pompidou Centre** is in Paris. All the walls are made of glass, built on a steel frame. A moving staircase goes all the way up the building, on the outside. Inside there are art galleries, a library and a cinema.

The **Sydney Opera House** is in Australia. It is built on land jutting out into Sydney Harbour. The roof is made of 10 shells. The highest shell is 75 metres (221 feet) above the water.

The tallest tower is in Toronto, Canada. It is the **Canadian National Tower**. It is 555 metres (1821 feet) tall.

Statues

The tallest statue in the world is in Russia. It is called **'Motherland'**. It is 82 m (270 feet) high.

The **Statue of Liberty** stands on Liberty island, at the entrance to New York harbour.

The **Great Buddha** is in Afghanistan. It was built by monks 1500 years ago.

The **Mount Rushmore Sculptures** in America are four giant heads each 18 m (60 ft) high. They are carved out of the rock. The faces are of four American presidents – George Washington, Thomas Jefferson, Theodore Roosevelt and Abraham Lincoln.

On **Easter Island**, in the Pacific Ocean, there are nearly 1000 statues. They are huge carved heads. It is believed that they are of their past chiefs. Three hundred of them are on platforms around the coast. All of these face inland.

Bridges

Sydney Harbour bridge is the widest long-span bridge in the world. It has two electric railway tracks, eight lanes of roadway, one cycle track and one footpath.

The **Lake Pontchartrain Causeway** is the longest bridge. It is near New Orleans in America. It is 38½ km (nearly 24 miles) long. It is so long that when you are in the middle you cannot see the land on either side.

The **Humber Bridge** in England has the longest gap between its main supports. The distance between the two towers is 1410m (4626 ft). Each tower rises to a height of 162m (530 ft). As the Earth's surface is curved, the towers are farther apart at the top than at the bottom.

Power and energy

Electricity is an important source of power and energy. It is made in many different ways. We can use water, the wind and the sun to make electricity.

The **Grand Coulee Dam** on the Columbia River, in Washington, USA, is the largest concrete dam in the world. It is 1272 m (4173 feet) long and 167 m (548 feet) high.

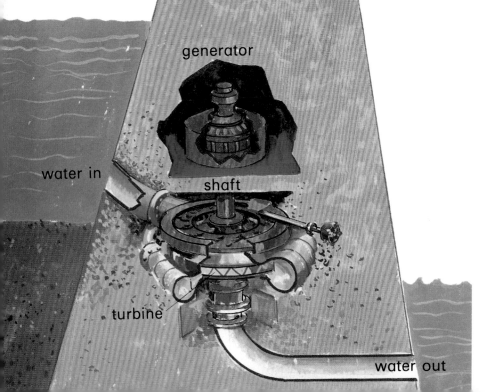

To make **electricity**, water from behind the dam rushes through pipes at the bottom. It moves so fast along the pipes that it makes a big wheel (turbine) spin. The turbine drives a machine called a generator. The generator makes electricity.

Many countries in the world are seeking other sources of power. This could be a **wind machine** of the future. It turns offshore winds into electricity. Each propeller is 18m (60 feet) long.

This **solar (sun) power station** at Odeillo makes electricity that is used all over France. The huge mirrors reflect sunlight on to a furnace. The temperature in the furnace reaches nearly 4000°C.

The **Rance Barrage** is a **tidal power station** in France. A huge wall (barrage) has been built across the mouth of the river. The tide rises and falls 13 m (42½ feet) every day. The water is used to drive underwater turbines to make electricity.

In the water

Oil rigs

Oil is very important to us. Sometimes it is called 'liquid gold'. No machine can work without oil. Oil is fuel for cars and trucks, aircraft and ships. It is used in factories and power stations, and for heating. Oil can be found under deserts, under snow and ice, and under the sea. Oil collects in pools, deep down under the earth. These are called wells.

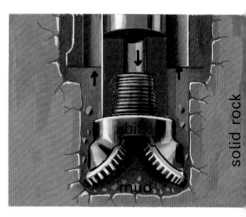

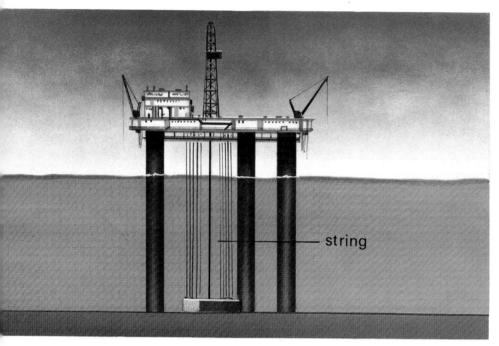

string

In the North Sea, **drilling rigs** work in water up to 300 m (1000 feet) deep. The oil can be another 3000 m (10,000 feet) under the seabed.

The drilling rig uses a drill to cut through the rock. The drill has a sharp tip at the end called a **bit**. The bit is studded with diamonds, which are the hardest stones.

The rest of the drill is called the **string**, which is a lot of metal pipes joined together. As the drill goes deeper, more pipes are added.

In very deep water, 6 km (3½ miles), a **drill ship** is used. The drilling bit and the drill string go down into the water, through a hole in the bottom of the ship.

A **support ship** guards the drill ship in the Arctic Ocean. Huge floating icebergs might crash into the drill ship. When an iceberg gets too near, a tow rope is fixed around the iceberg. Then it is towed out of the way. This ship can tow icebergs weighing up to 100 million tonnes.

When the drilling rigs have found oil a **production platform** is fixed into place. The drilling pipes pass down, inside the legs of the platform. As many as 40 wells can be drilled from one platform.

The oil now needs to be brought ashore. Sometimes it is piped to an **oil tanker** at sea, or it is carried in pipes under the sea to the shore.

Underwater craft

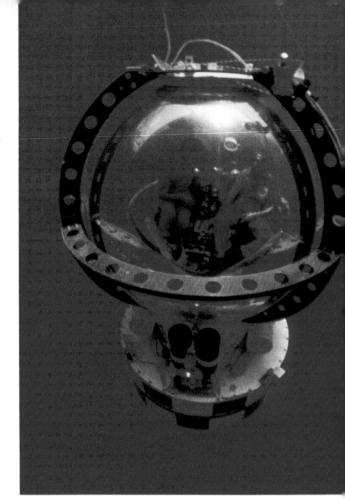

Submersibles are underwater craft. They are smaller than submarines and are carried on a ship. They are lowered into the sea. Special arms, cameras and equipment are fixed on to the outside.

'**NEMO**' has clear plastic walls. Two people can sit inside and watch underwater building and repair work. 'NEMO' has special electric plugs fitted on the outside, so that divers can use lights and power tools.

OBSS (Ocean Bottom Scanning Sonar vehicle) is another search vessel. It is pulled along the seabed by a cable attached to a ship on the surface. Robot machines are used when conditions are too dangerous for people. It is operated by remote control, from the ship above.

The 'Sea Cat' is used to bury
telephone cables under the seabed.
The cables are laid by cable ship,
but they could be damaged if they
rest on the bottom of the sea.
The 'Sea Cat' buries them under the
sand using special tools.

'Purisima' is a **bathysphere**. It is
an American craft built for underwater exploration. It is attached
by a cable to a ship on the surface.
There is also a telephone cable so
that people on the ship can talk to
the divers.

Bathyscaphe means 'deep
boat'. The 'Trieste' has
dived deeper than any
other craft, 11·3 km (7
miles). The crew sit in
the globe, underneath the
ship. They shine powerful
lights through the water.
Then they film through the
windows. The tanks above
are filled with petrol
and lead balls. These lead
balls help the craft to go
down. They are unloaded
into the sea when the
ship comes back up.

Special ships

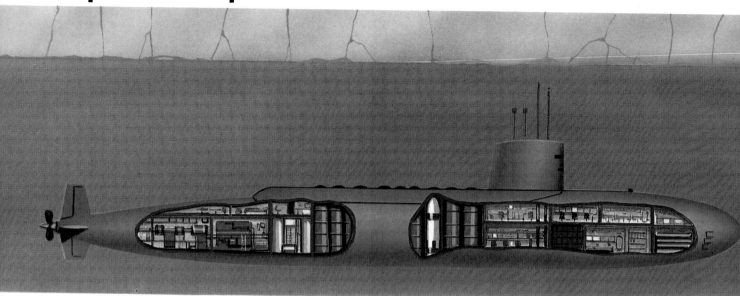

Submarines are big ships that travel under water. They are built with two hulls (bodies), one inside the other. Between the two hulls are ballast tanks. When these tanks are full of air, the submarine floats. When water is let into the tanks, the submarine gets heavier and sinks under water. The 'Nautilus', a nuclear submarine, was the first to travel under the ice at the North Pole.

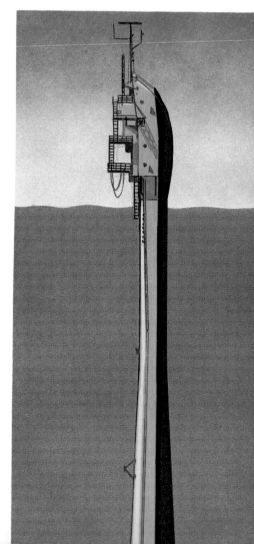

'**Flip**' is a floating instrument platform. It is a very long ship – 108 m (355 feet) – with no engines. It is towed out to sea. When it is in the right position, it is flooded so that one end sinks and the other end rises up out of the water. Scientists can walk down into the waterproof sections to study the sea and measure the waves.

The 'Shin Aitoku Maru' is a Japanese **sail-assisted tanker**. It has engines like most tankers, but it also has two sets of sails which increase its speed. The sails are 12 m (39 feet) high and 8 m (26 feet) wide.

A **pontoon** is a flat-bottomed boat, used for support. When a bridge has to be built in a hurry, it can be supported by a row of pontoons fixed to the riverbed. Armies use this method, because it is portable.

Sea lanes (routes) are sometimes blocked in bad weather by snow and ice. **Icebreakers** are strengthened ships used to break a path through the ice. The 'Manhattan', the largest icebreaker, is a converted supertanker.

Fire boats are used to put out fires in buildings near seas or on rivers. They have powerful engines to pump up the water to the hoses.

Rescue craft

The **Tyne class lifeboat** is used to save lives around the British coast. It is made of steel and aluminium and is 14·3 m (47 ft) long. It has a top speed of 18 knots. This boat cannot sink. If it is turned over by huge waves, it will come back upright within five seconds.

This **jetboat** is used in Bermuda for rescue work close to the shore, in shallow water and over coral reefs. There are no propellors which could get caught on the rocks and reefs. Its powerful diesel engines suck in sea water and force it out through jets. This pushes the boat forwards.

A **rescue hovercraft** is used by the Canadian Coast Guard. It is based at Vancouver airport. It can skim over floating logs and ice. In good weather it has a speed of 55–60 knots. It is the only hovercraft that is used for rescue work.

The 'John T Essberger' is a large German **rescue cruiser**. There is a small lifeboat, under a helicopter pad, at the stern (back) of the ship. It is 44·5 m (146 feet) long and has three powerful engines. It has a range of 966 km (600 miles) travelling at a speed of 30 knots.

A **rescue submarine** called 'DSRV' is used by the United States Navy. They provide a world-wide rescue service. The 'DSRV' can be carried in an aircraft to anywhere in the world within 24 hours of a disaster. The 'DSRV' is 15 m (49 feet) long and weighs 30 tonnes. It is designed to rescue crews from underwater craft, especially submarines. The bell-shaped skirt under the 'DSRV' fits over the escape hatch on the submarine. It can carry up to 24 people and go back many times, until everyone is safe.

Giants on the sea

The '**USS Enterprise**' is the world's largest warship. It is 336 m (1102 feet) long. It is a nuclear-powered ship and can travel very fast – 35 knots. This **aircraft carrier** is a floating base for up to 100 aircraft. There are 4600 members in the crew.

The '**Queen Elizabeth the Second (QE2)**' is a huge ocean liner, 293 m (962 feet) long. It is a luxury floating hotel which carries passengers on round-the-world cruises. It has 10 lifeboats on each side of the ship, a theatre, a cinema, a library and a swimming pool.

Water skimmers

This **hovercraft** does not have to push through the water. It hovers just above the surface. This makes it much faster, with a top speed of 65 knots. It skims over the water on a cushion of air. The air, made by powerful fans, is trapped under the craft by a skirt. The hovercraft can also travel on land, over soft mud, marsh and snow. The 'BHC Super 4' is the world's biggest hovercraft. It carries 416 passengers and 55 cars. Each of its four propellors is as high as a house.

A **hydrofoil** also skims above the water. When moving slowly, it travels through the water like a boat. As it gathers speed, it rises up on hydrofoils (underwater wings). This allows it to go faster than ordinary boats. It has a top speed of 80 knots. Because the hull (body) of the boat is above the water, it gives a smooth ride.

In the air

the cockpit of Concorde

Concorde is the fastest passenger airliner. It is powered by four Rolls Royce turbo jet engines that boost it to speeds of more than 2300 km/h (1450 mph). It has a needle-shaped nose and de Ha (triangular) shaped wings. The nose is lowered on take-off and landing, to give the pilot a better view of the runway.

The **'Super Guppy' (C-5A Galaxy)** is the world's largest aircraft. It was built to carry parts of space rockets and has a wing span of 43 m (141 ft). When it is loaded, a huge door in the nose swings open.

The **Boeing 747 'Jumbo Jet'** is the biggest airliner. It can carry 550 passengers and 17 crew. The main cabin is 60 m (197 feet) long and nearly 7 m (22 feet) wide.

Working aircraft

This is a **rainmaker aircraft**.
In countries where there is little rain, or a long drought, these planes are used to make it rain. They fly above the clouds and drop chemicals into the clouds. This releases the water in the clouds – and it rains.

The **'Canadian CL215' amphibious flying boat** has huge water tanks. They can hold 5455 litres (1200 gallons) of water. The tanks can be reloaded by the plane skimming across the surface of a lake.
It takes only 20 seconds to refill the tanks with water. The planes drop the water on forest fires.

On huge ranches in South America cattle may be scattered over many miles. **Light aircraft** like this one are used to track the herds at round-up time.

In the north of Canada, there are great areas of forest and many lakes. **Sea planes** fly in supplies to people living in remote places. They have special floats instead of wheels.

Special aircraft

The **Harrier Jump Jet** can hover, fly sideways and backwards. Unlike ordinary planes, this jet does not need a runway. It can take off, and land, vertically. The jet engines swivel and the force lifts the jet straight up into the air. It can fly at more than 1000 km/h (621 mph).

The **Lockheed Hercules** can fly on long-range journeys. Its vast tanks carry an enormous amount of fuel. This plane is often used to re-fuel smaller aircraft in mid-air. It can carry heavy loads of machinery or troops.

This is a **Japanese amphibian plane**. It is able to land on a runway or on water. The plane can take off, and land, in very rough seas. It is often used to rescue people in danger at sea.

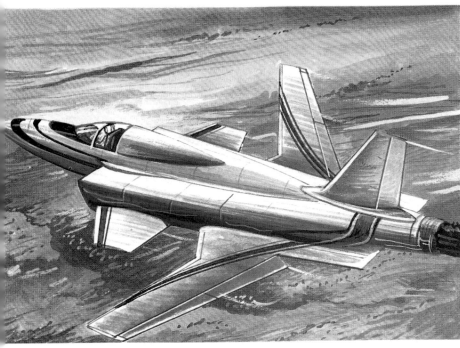

The **Grumman X-29A** is an American experimental plane. It has a new design with forward-sweeping wings. This plane is 15 m (48 ft) long. It can take off and land at lower speeds, on shorter runways, than other fighter aircraft.

The **American F 111** is a swing-wing aircraft. During take-off and landing the wings are fully opened out. As the plane increases speed in the air, the wings fold inwards. Now the plane can fly supersonic (faster than the speed of sound).

Helicopters

Helicopters do not need a runway, unlike most aircraft. They take off, and land, vertically. The engines turn the larger rotor blades (spinning wings) on top and this lifts the helicopter into the air. The smaller rotor blade on the tail is used for steering. They can hover, fly sideways and fly backwards.

This **Russian M1-2 helicopter** is used by the forest protection patrol. It can land anywhere, in a very small space. This helicopter is bringing in extra equipment to fight the fire.

The **autogyro** is different from a helicopter. The engine moves it forwards along the runway and the moving air spins the rotor blade. It cannot hover (stay still) in the air.

The **Sikorsky Sky Crane** is a huge American helicopter used for heavy lifting jobs. It can lift damaged aircraft or huge containers. The Sky Crane can carry 10 tonnes of cargo.

The **Apache** is the United States' newest helicopter. It is used by the Army as an advanced attack helicopte The Apache has special armoured protection and laser-guided weapons.

Telescopes and satellites

A **telescope** helps us to see far into Space. Inside it there are pieces of glass (lenses) and mirrors. These make stars and planets look bigger, and nearer, than they really are. The telescope can be moved to watch different parts of the sky. The pictures are shown on a screen.

This is a **communications satellite**. It can bounce radio and television signals from one side of the world to the other. Someone in Australia can watch what is happening on American television.

Earth seen from Space

This is a **weather satellite**. It orbits the Earth taking photographs, day and night, using special cameras. It can see how the clouds and winds move. The satellite can warn us of approaching storms.

Machines in Space

The **Space Shuttle** is the first re-usable space-craft. It is launched like a rocket, and flies back to Earth, to land like a plane. It is 37 m (121 feet) from nose to tail. It has delta wings, with a span of 24 m (79 feet). It has five computers on board.

When it is launched, two solid booster rockets and a huge fuel tank are bolted on to it.

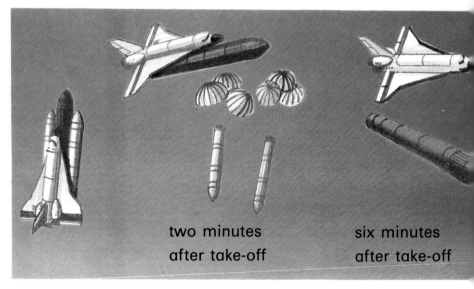

two minutes
after take-off

six minutes
after take-off

After two minutes' flight, the two solid booster rockets fall away. Six minutes later, at the edge of Space, the empty fuel tank falls away and burns up. The Shuttle's own three rocket engines carry it into Space, where it can stay for up to 30 days.

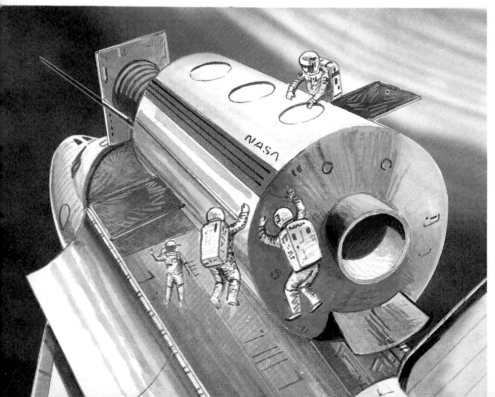

The Shuttle is used to launch new satellites and to repair broken ones. In the future it will carry **Spacelab** into orbit. Spacelab is being built by America, Canada, Japan and 11 European countries. It is a laboratory that fits into the Shuttle's cargo bay, where scientists will carry out experiments.

This special car was used by Amerian astronauts on the Moon. It is called **Lunar Rover Vehicle (LRV)** and is powered by electricity. There are two cameras on it.

The Russian moon car was called **Lunokhod 1**. It roamed over the Moon's surface for nearly a year, sending back photographs of the Moon. It was controlled by a radio on Earth.

Robot explorers

Mariner 9 was the first space probe to give us information about Mars. It sent back television pictures showing giant volcanoes on Mars.

The **Pioneer 10** space probe flew past Jupiter, taking many photographs. It took nearly two years to get there from Earth.

In the making

In Japan they are building a **double deck road–rail bridge**. It will link Honshú and Shikoku. The main span of the bridge will be 1780 m (5840 feet) It will also have side spans, which will make the whole bridge 3560 m (11,680 feet) long. It will be the longest bridge in the world.

The Russians are building a huge earth-filled dam, across the Vakhsh River. It will be called the **Rogunsky dam**. It will be the highest in the world, at 325 m (1066 feet) high. This is an artist's painting.

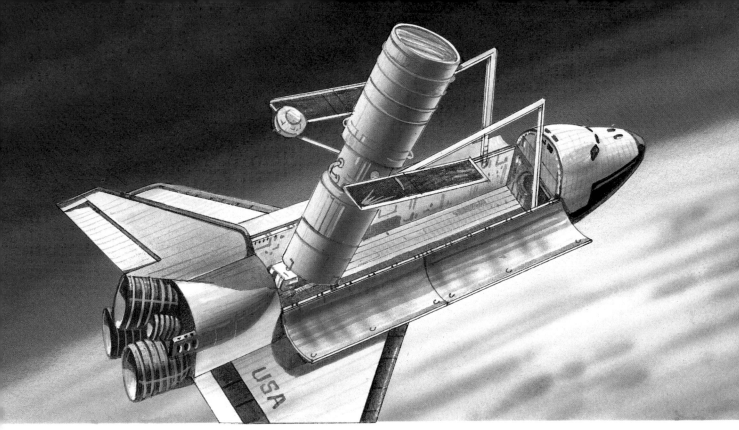

The United States is building a huge space telescope. It will
be 13 m (42½ ft) long and will weigh 10·9 tonnes. The **NASA
Space telescope** will see farther out into Space than any
telescope on Earth. It will be launched by the Space Shuttle.

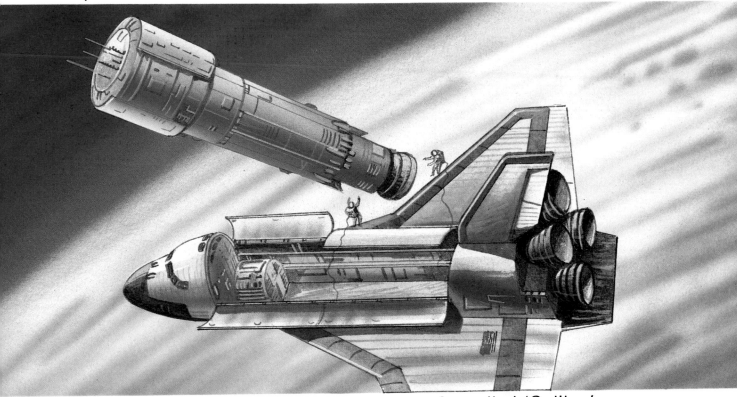

The Space Shuttle will launch a new **space probe** called 'Galileo'.
The Shuttle will carry it into orbit and it will be boosted on
its journey by a rocket. It will travel through space to explore
the giant planet Jupiter.